SELF-REGULATION LIFE WORKBOOK FOR KIDS

100+ Fun Activities, DBT Skills and CBT Exercises for Kids to Relieve Anxiety and Stress

By

S. Cooper

ATOM Publications

About the Author

S. Cooper is committed to giving parents, teachers, and mental health professionals the tools and techniques they need to help kids gain social and emotional skills. She likes to read books, watch basketball, enjoy the warm climate, and spend time with her family. She has participated in numerous community outreach initiatives as a strength-based trainer and educator due to her interest in comprehending children's emotions. She has worked with some of the most renowned and successful programs for young people, adolescents, and children. She has an advantage in child therapy because of her extensive training and experience as a teacher and a counselor. She is dedicated to comprehending how complicated children's emotions are, strategic Mindfulness practices, and effective anger management methods.

CONTENTS

INTRODUCTION

Warm and sincere connections help children learn self-control. They also learn it by observing the grownups in their immediate environment. Self-regulation in children begins when they are infants. The toddler and preschool years are when it develops the fastest, but it continues to grow up until adulthood. Babies, for instance, may suck their fingers for comfort or turn away from their caretakers if they are tired or need a break from their attention.

Toddlers are capable of waiting briefly for food and toys. However, young toddlers may steal items from other kids if they desire them. And tantrums occur when intense emotions overcome toddlers. In case of preschoolers, they begin to comprehend how to play with other kids and what is expected of them in social situations. For instance, a young child could attempt to speak softly if you are watching a movie.

Children of school age are becoming more adept at regulating their desires and demands, picturing other kids' viewpoints, and weighing all options. This suggests, for instance, that they might be able to argue with kids without getting into a fight. Preteens and adolescents are better at making plans, persevering through challenging activities, acting in a socially acceptable manner, and taking other kids' feelings into account.

Various factors may occasionally impact your child's capacity for self-regulation. For instance, your child's capacity to control their reactions and behavior might be impacted by fatigue, illness, and changes in routine. Additionally, some kids manage their behavior well in daycare, school, or sports but struggle to do so at home. Other kids suffer in crowded, boisterous environments like shopping malls. Additionally, self-regulation may become difficult as kids get older and have more evaluation duties or relationship issues.

Self-Regulation Life Workbook will help your child to learn coping skills and inform you more about your kids' problems and solutions. It's a great idea to talk with a specialist if you're concerned about your child's behavior or you're experiencing issues with your child's behavior as they become older, even though these self-regulation issues are very common. You could consult a doctor, a nurse specializing in children's and families' health, or an educator or child care provider for your child.

This book is for you if one of the following applies to your child:

- Your child appears to have more temper tantrums or challenging conduct than typical kids of his age.
- Your child is acting out of control or challenging more frequently as they age.
- Your child is acting in a way that could be harmful to them or others.
- Your kids Face challenges to discipline themselves.
- Your efforts to promote positive conduct don't appear to have any effect.
- Your child is highly reclusive and finds it difficult to interact with others.
- Your child doesn't appear to have as many communication and social skills as other kids of his age.

Worried about your kids? Here is a solution of all your worries and concerns regarding your kids. Follow me and I will help you.

A Note for Readers

Self-regulation is among the most crucial areas of skill development for children during the first five years of their lives. Our favorite definition of self-regulation comes from researchers, who define it as controlling thoughts and emotions to enable goal-directed behavior. Giving our children a strong foundation in self-regulation abilities is essential if we want them to plan, manage, and achieve their life goals successfully.

A child's capacity for self-regulation is their capacity to control their thoughts, emotions, and behaviors in a way that supports goal-directed conduct. Although self-regulation is sometimes thought of as a single talent, it may be helpful to further divide it into skill groups that include:

- Memorization, mental flexibility, and self-control are the mental abilities that make up executive function. Setting and achieving objectives is correlated with these abilities.
- A set of mental techniques and behaviors for controlling strong or uncomfortable emotions, including anger, irritation, excitement, worry, or stress. These abilities are linked to the ability to calm oneself down, soothe others, and deal with ambiguity in one's environment.
- A set of mental abilities that enable a child to participate in healthy actions and avoid bad habits to control their negative emotions is known as behavioral regulation. These abilities are linked to the ability to control one's behavior in the classroom, restrain undesirable behavioral inclinations, and concentrate on goal achievement.

Self-regulation is crucial to a child's growth, and its significance cannot be overstated. Children who develop self-control have a higher chance of doing well in school, staying out of trouble, and achieving their long-term objectives as they age. They are more robust, less resistant to external changes, and better at handling stress and annoyance. Additionally, they perform things more effectively and are better at concentrating, shifting their attention when necessary, and functioning in groups.

According to studies, stronger self-regulation abilities formed early in childhood are key predictors of academic success, interpersonal connections, and reducing behavioral issues later in life.

Every child differs when it comes to basic behavioral and emotional self-regulation. Children naturally differ in their early self-regulation abilities for genetic and biological causes that child development scientists have thoroughly documented.

However, with the right mix of motivation/incentives, caregiving support, and suitable environmental/structural background, behavioral and emotional self-regulation are abilities that can be taught via direct teaching and intentional practice, just like how to count, write, or spell.

Both factors matter when weighing nature vs. nurture in the context of self-regulation. The innate tendencies of a youngster determine their starting position on the race track in the quest to develop these essential talents. Some youngsters get off to a faster start than others, and vice versa. While some may need more one-on-one assistance than others, all may cross the finish line with the right instruction and care from caregivers.

This book will focus on the significance of self-regulation to children's education and development. We'll look at self-regulation, its components, how it develops and manifests in kids of different ages, and how families and daycare providers can encourage self-regulation in young children's development.

PART-I

(MANAGE THOUGHTS, FEELINGS AND ACTIONS THROUGH CBT)

Chapter 1: The Magic Triangle of CBT

Hey Parents/Teachers/Caregivers!

Kids often have unpleasant thoughts in their minds. We search for issues so that we can be prepared for them. We punish ourselves because we do not wish to keep repeating the same mistakes. However, this propensity for pessimistic thought usually works against us. Instead, it increases the likelihood of feeling negative about ourselves, making us less generally joyful. Therapists and other professionals use the CBT triangle, often the cognitive triangle, to explain the idea of altering unfavorable thought patterns. The triangle's points illustrate the interconnectedness of thoughts, emotions, and behaviors. You can improve the other two by improving one of these three points.

Employing the Tool

Millie learnt English at a nearby high school. She used to like performing in regional plays and was eager to try out for the upcoming performance. She was rejected at the final call-back for her last two auditions.

After this setback, Millie believed she must not be smart or beautiful enough. She kept telling herself she wouldn't succeed even though she wanted to participate in the show. She decided against going since she was disheartened.

She used this choice to criticize herself and reminded herself that she would never succeed as an actor. The cycle kept going.

This would look like this in the CBT triangle cycle:

- I don't think I'm talented enough to be an actress

- Discouragement and self-doubt
- Behavior: Complete lack of effort

Millie might be able to shield herself from more disappointment by giving up. And she continued in this destructive loop by refusing to challenge her ideas. Millie had decided that she didn't know to be correct and hadn't looked at any other options. She would have to think about fresh perspectives on her circumstance to question the preconceived notions. The following information regarding the situation could contradict her conclusion:

- Despite not selecting her for prior roles, the local theater's director was supportive when she first tried out.
- Because she didn't truly fit the characters in the past, Millie felt she would not be suitable for those roles.
- Her strengths were considerably better suited to the new play.
- Millie was aware of additional talented players who, depending on the production, were not always get cast.
- Millie had only done a few auditions, but she knew that most performers were rejected numerous times before being cast.
- Millie frequently heard in college that she was a good performer.
- Millie could take into account all of this data collection. Millie chose to give a new idea some thought after giving it some thought and chatting to a friend about it.

New Thought: I've had positive comments in the past regarding my acting. I was encouraged to reapply by the director.

New emotion: Excited, awaiting

Changing behavior: Getting ready for the role and attending the audition

No one can say for sure if Millie landed the role. Trying something new and putting ourselves out there might be frightening. However, we also understand that if she continued her destructive behavior, she would never get better and probably regret not trying.

Employing the CBT triangle is a continuous activity. Millie would probably also need to confront other self-defeating thoughts. But with time and effort, Millie could begin to break the habit of purposefully sabotaging her aspirations. Her mind would eventually stop instinctively going to the negative thought. She would get a more optimistic outlook on life.

Even if performing wasn't in Millie's future, this might help her discover activities she liked that made her happy. She might even become the play's leading lady! She was determined that the danger was worthwhile.

1.1 Thoughts, Feelings, Actions

Hey kids!

The Cognitive Triangle manifests itself in our daily lives as follows:

You feel worn out, sleepy, and uneasy when you wake up. You detest giving speeches in front of crowds, but today you have a lengthy presentation.

"I'm going to screw up," "No one is going to enjoy my speech," "I can't even talk in front of a gathering; how am I likely to accomplish anything?" "I'm worthless," "I'm a loser," and "I should just stay in the house, so I don't make a fool of myself" are some of your first thoughts. The internal dialogue we conduct with ourselves is frequently composed of these notions. How many hours have you ended up finding yourself saying something similar?

Here come the emotions. You're feeling even worse following a morning of verbal abuse from within. You are dreading giving your upcoming presentation. In general, you feel awful about yourself, and being present is the last thing you wish to do. Let's take a moment to stand back. Is it surprising that our thoughts have such a strong impact on how we feel? It matters what we tell ourselves.

Now the behavior appears. You finally leave after much back-and-forth and procrastination, and you're just starting your presentation. Your mind is racing as you start, and your level of anxiety is unchanged. Even if you are quite knowledgeable about the topic of your presentation, you find it difficult to express your ideas clearly. You struggle to finish your speech, tripping over your words and failing to tie together the ideas you labored so hard to develop. You choked on using the common language. How often have we performed this? We get so worked up over something normally well within our abilities that we can hardly get through it.

Your confidence took yet another hit after this presentation. This incident appears to validate all of your self-deprecating ideas.

The cycle continues, and continues. and continues….

1.2 How Can We Modify Our Thoughts?

Any change doesn't happen until we shed light on this process and start to break the pattern. This is the main area of concentration in therapy. The transition is challenging rather than effortless. It takes a lot of hard work over a long time to break this pattern and teach healthy ways of thinking, feeling, and behaving because our brains grow adapted to how we have always done things.

If you can connect to this vicious cycle, know that you are not alone. All of us have encountered this procedure in some way or the other. It could be time to act, though, if you believe it impacts your life and general well-being. You don't have to do it alone; counseling is a terrific approach to understanding your inner dialogue and how it affects your moods and behavior.

1.3 How the Triangle Relates to CBT

A cognitive triangle is a tool used by cognitive behavioral therapists to demonstrate to their kids how their ideas, feelings, and behaviors may be changed to affect their environment. Anxiety and sadness are two mental health conditions that this method can help with.

Writing down all the negative thoughts that arise throughout the day and categorizing them by the triangle's sides can help patients keep control of their thoughts. They will be better able to identify thought patterns and triggers as a result, and they will be able to start avoiding them.

Although it may seem simple to describe and categorize emotions, there are frequently underlying emotions linked to the ones experienced at the time. The fear of losing a loved one may be the root of emotions like the rage. Finding the underlying feeling behind this will result in a completely different response, and combating mental health disorders depends on doing so.

Individual's actions change when they identify underlying feelings and alter their thinking. By advising them on behavioral adjustments, you can assist in influencing ideas and feelings.

Chapter 2: CBT for Anxiety and

Depression

Hey Parents/Teachers/Caregivers!

Anxiety and depression, the most prevalent type of mental illness that affect one-third of American kids, can be effectively treated using Cognitive Behavioral Therapy (CBT). Finding workable answers to an individual's anxiety-related triggers and symptoms is the main goal of CBT therapy.

CBT is an evidence-based treatment for some of the most prevalent behavioral and emotional problems. Still, it has been discovered to be particularly successful in treating anxiety disorders. CBT is the only therapy with as much evidence demonstrating its efficacy, making it commonly regarded as the "gold standard" in anxiety therapies.

CBT treats anxiety by assisting kids in altering their thoughts and behaviors when they are anxious. CBT seeks to assist individuals in stopping and altering the anxious thoughts that fuel anxiety while also assisting in lowering avoidant actions. Together, these adjustments lower the burden on their everyday lives and assist in reducing anxiety symptoms without the need for medication.

2.1 Activities for Anxiety and Depression

The following are some of the typical CBT methods for treating anxiety and depression symptoms:

Challenging Thoughts

By listing evidence for the concept's truth or falsity or evaluating plausible alternative explanations, one can challenge a thought to see if it is accurate. In times of stress or worry, challenging anxious thoughts might help lessen anxiety and unreasonable and impulsive judgments.

For instance, one typical CBT technique for addressing illogical thinking is to list the facts supporting and refuting a certain notion or assumption. This ability can assist kids in recognizing when their thoughts may be skewed as a result of their fear as opposed to accepting them as fact.

Thought Stopping

Once kids know their patterns, CBT therapists may start teaching them techniques to break up and replace some behaviors. Many CBT techniques concentrate on assisting kids in interrupting troublesome cognitive patterns, but some also concentrate on assisting kids in interrupting unhelpful behavioral habits. Once these patterns are disrupted, the kids learn how to replace them with more advantageous ones.

The ability to stop thoughts entails giving them a verbal or visual mental command to halt whenever unproductive ones arise. When someone starts to repeat an embarrassing incident or worry about something that hasn't yet happened, they may use the word "Stop" or "No," or they may visualize the image of a stop sign.

Changing How You Think

Reframing is a skill that entails stopping an unproductive idea and attempting to reframe it more beneficially. For instance, a kid can reframe a worry about an impending doctor's appointment by considering how it might improve their health.

Reframing can assist kids in changing their way of thinking to feel less anxious and respond more effectively when a kid's thinking has become overemotional; reframing aids in reintroducing more logical thought habits.

Pattern Recognition

CBT therapy aims to increase functioning while reducing symptoms by altering thought and behavior patterns. Early treatment frequently focuses on assisting kids in identifying these patterns and figuring out how to stop them before they become troublesome to support the achievement of that objective.

Typical CBT assignments contain logs that ask customers to record these:

- They have various thoughts throughout the day, particularly when they feel stressed or anxious.
- Emotions they feel and how strongly they feel them.
- Anxiety-related actions and reactions, as well as any negative or positive results they may have.
- Either internally or externally, circumstances elicit a particular set of ideas, feelings, and reactions.

Explicit Tasks

Exposure assignments are frequently advised to limit avoidance, reduce anxiety, and boost confidence in anxious kids since they tend to avoid circumstances that make them feel uneasy. Exposure exercises entail gradually exposing oneself to dreaded circumstances and progressing to more deeply feared and avoided circumstances.

For instance, a kid who is averse to public speaking can begin by rehearsing in front of one or two acquaintances before moving on to a small group at work. To help kids prepare for these exposures, CBT therapists frequently teach their patients relaxation techniques like deep breathing or muscular relaxation. Exposures give kids the confidence to face their anxieties and the tools to do so while improving their anxiety management techniques.

Below are some worksheets that will help kids to overcome their anxiety and depression.

My Anxiety

Use this worksheet to explore more about how you respond to anxiety!

Things that make me feel anxious!

Thoughts that go through my head....

How my body responds when I'm anxious

ANXIETY PREP

It can be helpful to be prepared when you are going into a situation that might make you feel anxious or nervous. Use this worksheet to figure out things that you can do before and during the situation to help you cope if you become anxious.

WHATS THE SITUATION?

WHAT MIGHT MAKE ME FEEL ANXIOUS?

WHAT THINGS CAN I SAY OR DO BEFORE TO PREPARE FOR THIS SITUATION?

HOW HAVE I HANDLED IT BEFORE?

HOW WILL I KNOW THAT I'M GETTING ANXIOUS?

COPING SKILLS I CAN USE IF I START TO FEEL ANXIOUS?

25

I Can Cope

I Can Cope! with feeling ANXIOUS

Some things that make me feel anxious are....

1._____

2._____

3._____

These changes happen when I feel anxious:

Changes in my body...	Thoughts I have....	Things I do....

When I feel anxious. I can cope by:

Check all of the coping skills that might be helpful! Use the blank spaces to write in your own.

☐ Deep breathing   ☐ Going for a walk   _____

☐ Use positive self-talk   ☐ Writing in my journal   _____

☐ Meditating or relaxing ☐ Practicing mindfulness   _____

☐ Talking to a friend   ☐ Thinking happy thoughts   _____

☐ Talking to an adult   ☐ Keeping my self busy   _____

☐ Playing a game   ☐ Exercising   _____

How I Feel

I feel: _____

Happy	Mad	Sad	Glad
Worried	Excited	Bored	Scared
Annoyed	Upset	Sick	Nervous

I feel this way because:

_____

_____

_____

This is what I did about it:

_____

_____

_____

Something else I could have done is:

_____

_____

_____

Ask for help	Take deep breaths	Walk away
Do something else	Tell an adult	Talk to a friend

How Depression Feels in my Body

Color in the feelings you have in your body when you feel depressed.

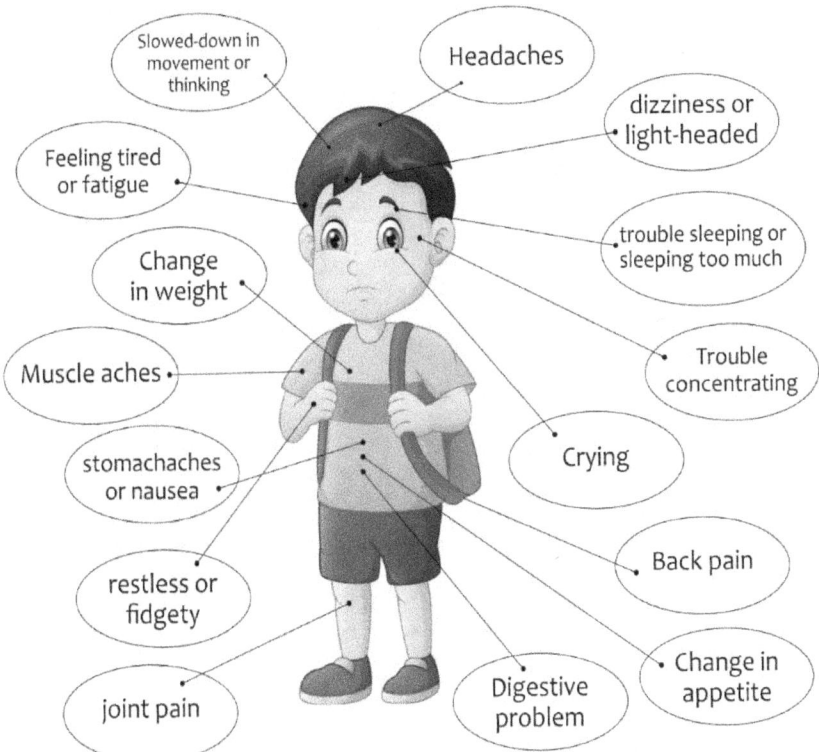

What other symptoms do you experience when you feel depressed?

1._____

2._____

3._____

Chapter 3: Overcome Fears and Worries

with CBT

Hey Kids!

Many of us appreciate the scary movies, creepy literature, and festive decor during the Halloween season. We highlight the feeling of fear and being terrified at this time of year. But most kids don't fear vampires, goblins, or monsters. In our everyday lives, we are more frequently faced with the fears of failure, rejection, and missing out. Fear can hold you back from living your best life and achieving your full potential. Some of us could dread particular circumstances, things, or people. We could experience challenges in our day-to-day activities and the pursuit of our objectives if we strive to avoid these triggers.

Potential threat or warning triggers the strong emotion of fear. This feeling brings on different behavioral and physiological changes. Feelings like anger, despair, and shame may be brought on. We may respond to this sensation by avoiding or facing the imagined threat. The fight-or-flight response is what is meant by this. Additionally, this reaction may result in uncontrollable physical symptoms such as a faster heartbeat, clammy, sweaty palms, dizziness, and frequent urine. As a result, your anxiety symptoms may worsen since you may feel ill or in danger.

The Purpose of Fear

Fear is an excellent emotion to have. It's the body's way of alerting us that potential harm to our safety. While fear can often be a good and safe reaction, there are other circumstances in which it is less beneficial. Fear can keep us from learning crucial life lessons in these circumstances. For instance, you might decide not to apply for the audition of school play you want out of fear of rejection. Your fears connected to social anxiety may keep you from making new friends and developing connections. If you dread confrontation, standing up for yourself in unfair circumstances could be difficult.

An overwhelming and persistent fear of certain things or circumstances is referred to as a phobia, a sort of anxiety condition. Kids with a phobia will go to any lengths to avoid the things they are afraid of. If they can't avoid the trigger, it will cause them much distress.

Cognitive Behavioral Therapy for Managing Fear

CBT also called cognitive behavioral therapy, is a relatively new psychotherapy approach. It focuses on questioning problematic thinking patterns, attitudes, and cognitive distortions to change them. Through exposure therapy, CBT pushes you to confront your concerns in the real world. It has been proven that this works on many individuals, including those with severe phobias and social anxiety. By gradually exposing patients to the source of their anxiety, exposure therapy enables them to "climb the fear ladders."

For instance, a patient who fears spiders could first view photographs of spiders before viewing a film. They can watch a spider in a confined location from a distance when they are ready to do so. They'll become closer and closer as time passes. They might one day succeed in managing a spider with just their hands. Of course, this happens gradually over a long period, and at speed the patient can bear. This can work against you if your exposures are too great.

Similarly, those who struggle with social anxiety might start by smiling at a stranger on their walk to work each day and work their way up to striking up a discussion with someone there. They might eventually have the self-assurance to pursue a love interest. Years of study have demonstrated that the signs of anxiety significantly lessen over time if we consciously and methodically face our concerns.

3.1 Activities to Overcome Fears

The greatest approach to overcoming those ingrained concerns is to confront them head-on. This is a normal and fundamental aspect of human growth. Fortunately, thriving at this developmental stage is amazingly easy, available, and cost-free! Here are straightforward tips that young kids can use to face their fears head-on and develop their resilience, confidence, and ability to handle anxiety.

Engage in mindfulness. What precisely is mindfulness, which you may have heard of? Being mindful is passive thinking that helps you become more conscious of your fear. Practice mindfulness techniques during some of your less severe moments of fear and anxiety. Sit down and reflect on what is occurring to you as soon as you notice the signs of your dread beginning to emerge. This is like writing in a journal in your head. Watch the signs as they appear. Don't take any action. Sit and remain aware of yourself during the situation. Being passive makes you more conscious of yourself and keeps you from acting out of habit when you're afraid. It aids in breaking out of a rut.

Become informed. Nothing terrifies us more than the unknown. Get the information you need to evaluate the issue based on facts rather than conjecture if your worry is based on a lack of information.

Become more proportional. How significant is the thing you're terrified about? Sometimes, we become so preoccupied with a quest's success or failure that we lose sight of how it relates to everything else we hold dear. What is the worst that may happen? You could ask. Even while the reality isn't always good, you can discover that your worry is often worse than what you're worried will happen.

Get support. Do you need to face your fears alone, whatever they may be? Can you locate a mentor or a group of friends to lend support? Sport kids have coaches. Teachers work with students. Friends can occasionally offer the support you need to tackle your fear, even if they lack competence in the subject you're having trouble with.

Instead of just acting, remain motionless! We often look up to those who are fast to act, yet taking your time, planning, and being deliberate are also important acts. Haste alone has jeopardized or destroyed many successful endeavors. When anxiety overtakes you, think about whether the best course of action could be to weigh your alternatives carefully and make an informed decision rather than acting on impulse.

Make use of peer pressure. Have you ever acted recklessly just because your buddies encouraged you, such as jumping over a high bridge into a river below? Like fear, peer influence can have a beneficial or harmful effect depending on how it is applied. Be in the company of kids who will encourage you to face your fears and achieve your goals.

Imagining success. Before accomplishing a physical goal, athletes may visualize it hundreds of times in their minds. Because of this mental mapping, the body is more likely to move along the predetermined course. The same routine will equip you to succeed in whatever goal.

Role-play, practice, and prepare. Public speaking has long been considered the greatest fear in the US. In many surveys, speaking in front of a group of kids comes in second to death itself. Prepare, practice, and act out your fear if it has to do with how you will perform in a certain activity.

Accept fear and learn to live with it. It is fear that keeps us safe. It is a tool we can use to improve our decisions, not something that is necessarily good or evil. Fear encourages us to behave in ways that produce the outcomes we need and want, not ones that keep us passive. Accept fear as a teacher and allow it to guide rather than dictate your behavior.

Take a long view. You frequently worry that they won't be able to pay more attention to your studies or doing your best in exams. But what do you think will happen next? The short-term issue won't be resolved by thinking about it in the long run, but doing so can help you approach it more objectively and find the best answer.

Solve these worksheets below in order to overcome your fears.

My Fears

My Fears

What are some things
that make you feel
nervous or scared?

_____

_____

_____

What do you think about when you are nervous or scared? _____

_____

How does your body feel when you are nervous or scared? Color the areas
where you can sense these feelings.

What's something you can do to feel better next time you are afraid?

_____

Fear Ladder

Fear Ladder Worksheet

Pick a situation that you commonly avoid due to anxiety and uncomfortable feelings. Write it down below next to # 5 at the top of your ladder. Think of other smaller steps you can take to expose yourself to the fear you listed at the top of your ladder. Rate each step with the intensity of anxiety it would cause you to complete. Remember you want each step to cause some level of anxiety. Once you decide to work on your ladder you can start at the bottom and move up. or you\ can randomly pick any step and practice over and over.

1
2
3
4
5

Fears Crushing Worksheet

FEAR CRUSHING WORKSHEET

My Core Fear

Break down the fear into manageable parts

How can / will challenge that fear?

I'll repeat this affirmation when I'm facing my fear

I want to accomplish this more than I am scared of it

I'll use these resources to crush my fear

3.2 Activities to Tackle Worries

Doubts, fears, and worries are common aspects of existence. Being anxious is normal before important events like first day at school, admission interviews, and toy bills. But when worry is overwhelming and continuous, it stops being "natural" and becomes excessive. You constantly worry about "what ifs" and the worst-case situations, and this anxiety is interfering with your daily life.

Your physical and emotional health may suffer if you worry constantly, think negatively, or always assume the worst. It can deplete your emotional stamina, make you jittery and restless, give you headaches, stomachaches, and muscle strain, and make it difficult for you to focus at work or school. You might vent your bad sentiments on your loved ones, use alcohol or drugs as self-medication, or try to divert yourself by losing yourself in technology. Generalized Anxiety Disorder (GAD), a prevalent anxiety disorder that causes tension, anxiousness, and a general sense of unease that permeates your entire life, can also cause chronic worrying.

Being distracted from work, education, or your personal life by anxiety and concern makes it difficult to be productive in your everyday tasks. Here, the technique of delaying your worries can be beneficial.

Permit yourself to have an uncomfortable thought but postpone thinking about it until later rather than trying to suppress or get rid of it.

Worry Period. Set aside a specific time and location to worry. It should occur consistently each day (for example, from 5:10 to 5:30 p.m. in the sitting room) and early enough to prevent anxiety before bed. You are permitted to worry about anything during your worry period. However, the remainder of the day is anxiety-free.

Put your problems in writing. Make a quick note of any worrying or nervous thoughts that come to mind throughout the day, and then go about your normal activities. Remind yourself that you can think about it more later and don't need to worry about it now. Additionally, writing down your thoughts—whether on paper, a phone, or a computer—takes considerably more effort than simply thinking about them, which increases the likelihood that your anxieties will lose some of their stings.

During the worrying period, go over your "*concern list*." If the ideas you put down are still bugging you, permit yourself to worry about them, but only for the allotted time. When you evaluate your issues in this manner, you'll frequently discover that generating a more impartial viewpoint is simpler. Cut your worry time short and continue enjoying the remainder of your day if your troubles appear unimportant.

Break the worrying loop. When you worry too much, it may appear that your mind is spinning nonstop with bad ideas. Under all this tension, you could feel like you're losing control, going mad, or on the verge of exhaustion. However, there are actions you can take right away to put a stop to all those worrisome thoughts and give yourself a break from constant worrying.

Get up and move around. Exercise releases endorphins, which reduce tension and stress, increase energy, and improve your well-being. This makes exercise a natural and effective anti-anxiety medication. More significantly, you may stop the steady stream of worries flowing through your thoughts by paying close attention to how your body feels while you move. Pay attention to your breathing pattern, the rhythm of your steps, the feel of the sun or breeze on your skin, or the sound of your feet striking the ground as you run, walk, or dance, for instance.

Attend a class of yoga. Yoga and tai chi maintain your focus in the present by concentrating on your breath and motions, which helps to cleanse your mind and promote relaxation.

Meditate. When you meditate, your attention shifts from worrying about the future or reflecting on the past to what is happening right now. Being present can stop the never-ending cycle of anxious thoughts and fears. Additionally, there is no requirement for you to chant, light some candles, or sit cross-legged. Pick one of the many affordable or free smartphone applications that can assist you through breathing after finding a quiet, comfortable area.

Exercise gradual muscular relaxation. Directing your attention away from your thoughts and toward your body can assist you in breaking the cycle of anxiety. You can relieve stress in your muscles by alternately tensing and then relaxing various muscle groups. Your mind will follow your body's relaxation as well.

Aim to breathe deeply. Worrying causes you anxiety and makes you breathe more quickly, which frequently causes more anxiety. However, you may silence your bad emotions and relax your mind by engaging in deep breathing exercises.

Use the following worksheets to work on your worries.

Write down things and thoughts about which you are worried.

What am I worried about?

My Worry Cup

Now, put all your worries into this worry cup.

 # My Worry Cup

Directions Show how full your cup is with worry. Draw water drops to show how big your worries are. Little drops are little worries Big drops are big worries.

PART-II

(Regulate Emotions and Behaviors

through DBT)

Chapter 4: Emotions Regulation: Learn to

Let Go

Hey Kids!

Dialectical behavior therapy (DBT) uses the ability of emotion regulation to help us comprehend the purpose of emotions, the action drive that goes along with each feeling, and whether to heed or resist these urges. The following abilities also lessen susceptibility, boost resistance to unwelcome emotions, and enhance general mental wellness. Emotional control lessens susceptibility to undesirable emotions and boosts emotional toughness when they do. Emotion regulation techniques are preventative; however, DBT incorporates other skills like distress tolerance to help you manage challenging emotions.

4.1 What is Emotional Regulation?

Emotion regulation is a key component of dialectical behavior therapy (DBT), which teaches patients how to control strong, unpleasant emotions while enhancing their good ones. Three objectives are covered in this module:

- Recognize one's feelings
- Lessen emotional sensitivity
- Lessen the emotional pain

Understanding that unpleasant feelings are not harmful or something that has to be avoided is a key component of emotion control. Although they are a natural part of life, there are ways to acknowledge them before letting them go.

Kids who are extremely sensitive to emotions frequently go through cycles that start with an occurrence that sets off unwarrantedly negative thoughts. These feelings then cause an excessive or negative emotional reaction, which may ultimately result in disastrous behavioral decisions. Additional negative feelings like shame and self-loathing come after the harmful behavior.

Understanding Our Emotions

Every feeling you feel, has a particular function. You can learn about your current position from these feelings. We frequently refer to this as our "gut instinct." An illustration of this may be meeting a stranger who initially appears to be completely decent. But for some reason that you can't quite put your finger on, you feel anxious. Your emotions tell you something is awry when you have this reaction. Although emotions are not always reliable judges of your circumstances, paying attention to them is necessary. Furthermore, verbally or nonverbally, emotions show those around us how we feel (such as facial expressions). Determine the emotion you're experiencing and think about what it might be attempting to teach you about your circumstance.

Our emotions can influence the people around us to feel the same way. A supportive friend can help a person feel better when they are hurt. On the other hand, if we vehemently disseminate tales and gossip about someone, people who hear them could likewise start to feel unfavorable about that.

Our emotional experience might be so rapid in some situations, like a "fight or flight" scenario, that we don't mentally absorb what happens until after it has already happened. This occurs due to emotions' additional role in motivating particular responses or reactions from us. Our bodies naturally try to protect us from potentially harmful situations.

When you become aware of an emotion, watch it without passing judgment. Even if certain feelings could be more pleasant than others, they are all worthwhile. Determine the emotion you're experiencing and think about what it might be attempting to teach you about your circumstance. You can then choose whether to give in to the emotion or let it go at that point.

Decreasing Emotional Suffering

Reducing emotional distress is the DBT's final component, and it consists of two skills:

- Giving up
- Doing the opposite

Letting go is not avoiding, meditating on, or battling the current emotion but rather becoming attentive to it, acknowledging it, and then letting it go. Releasing a breath and imagining the thought or feeling drifting away or imagining the emotion as a tide can help with this.

Taking the reverse effect refers to acting in a way that would be normal when one is experiencing the opposite of the current emotion. For instance, a kid who is depressed can attempt acting energetically, standing tall, and speaking authoritatively—as they would if they were cheerful. When someone is angry, they will act calmly by speaking softly and doing kind deeds for others as if they were not angry. This technique encourages the kids to name their feeling and let them go, not to deny their current experience. However, the length and intensity of the unpleasant feelings will probably be reduced if the opposite is done.

Those who are not familiar with dialectical behavior therapy could find some of the emotion-regulation techniques a little hazy. DBT practitioners go into greater detail about these techniques with kids in group meetings, using role-playing to help the kids apply the new techniques to their life circumstances. Ultimately, these abilities enable kids to control their emotions instead of allowing them to control them.

My Emotions

I allow all my emotions to be here.

My rainbow of feelings that bursts from my sun is made up of many colours.
Colour and write a feeling word in each rainbow beam below:

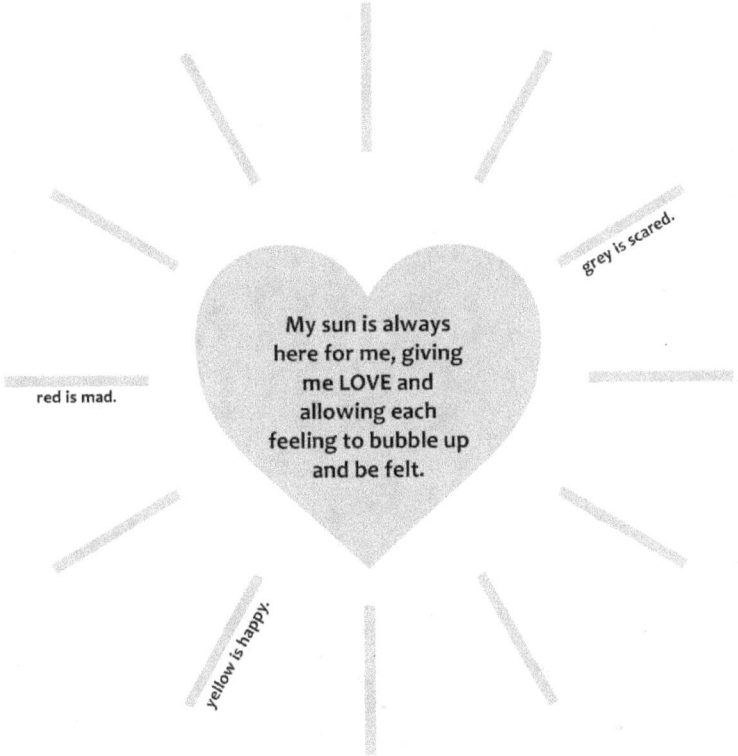

grey is scared.

red is mad.

My sun is always here for me, giving me LOVE and allowing each feeling to bubble up and be felt.

yellow is happy.

To try to feel only happy all the time is impossible because there are so many other colours to a rainbow!

53

Rocket Triggers

This bothers me a lot. I want it to explode

This bothers me a little bit

This does not bother me at all

54

My Feelings

How are you feeling today?

Today, I am feeling

I am feeling this way because.....

_____

_____

Some things I can do to help myself feel
better are....

1. _____

2. _____

3. _____

Some things others can do to help me feel
better are....

1. _____

2. _____

Right now, I need _____

Draw a picture of what your face
looks like today

When I Feel Sad

WHEN I FEEL SAD

I THINK....
(What are some thoughts that go through your head whenever you feel sad?)

I SAY....
(What are some things you say to other whenever you feel sad?)

I DO....
(What behavior do you display whenever you feel sad?)

_____   _____

_____   _____

My Feelings This Week

Write in the box times when you have experienced each of these emotions during the week. Share with others.

Angry

Sad

Happy

Scared

4.3 Emotions Regulation Games and Exercises

Games help youngsters gain social and emotional skills, according to studies. Emotional and social learning, two mechanisms that regulate emotions, are essential for emotion control. Psychologists and psychiatrists claim that depending on kids' attitude and disposition, some games may be more beneficial than others. Ability levels, behavioral manifestations, and emotional expressions are all influenced by the particular illness or handicap. The following major games are excellent picks to start with if you're seeking for games to assist with emotional processing:

"Emotions" Easter Egg Hunt

Easter egg hunts should not be reserved only for special occasions. Preparing the silicone eggs and concealing them both require some preparation for this exercise. The enjoyment in this game comes from locating the eggs and using emotional regulation abilities to solve problems. For this game, you'll need a couple of containers or boxes, some fake eggs, and a marker pen.

Each egg will have a different emotion-filled face painted on it. On the egg tops, draw various eyes and facial gestures; on the bottom, draw various mouths. Ask the participants to locate the eggs and identify the emotion displayed on each one.

Once they've decided on an emotion, ask them to put it in a container that matches the colors and meaning of the stoplights.

- *Green*

Happiness, pleasure, contentment, and focus are examples of positive emotions classified as green because they are peaceful feelings acceptable in most social contexts.

◀ *Yellow*

Approaching these emotions with caution is advised because they are slightly heightened. They frequently coincide with feelings of uneasiness, trepidation, or irritation.

◀ *Red*

Intense emotions are sensations of hatred, panic, or anger and are frequently accompanied by outbursts or tantrums.

◀ *Blue*

Here, sensations of sadness or boredom that lack vigor or intensity are classified.

Participants can reposition the eggs' tops and bottoms to create new feelings after mixing up the bottoms and tops to create them. The original ones will be color-congruent but difficult to match with so many eggs.

Freeze Dance

Self-control and the capacity to regulate your physical and mental states are also intimately related to emotional regulation. Even though it may not seem like it, this game encourages children to control their emotions better while having fun! For a short period, you can play this easy game to highlight having control over your body and emotions.

You merely need the ability to pause often and resume your music. Even if it's a sibling or another parent, playing this game with additional kids might make it more entertaining for the kids.

The youngster will be urged to walk around and dance when the music is on. They should be able to express happiness and joy as a result. Everyone taking part should freeze and return to a peaceful and serious mindset as soon as the music finishes.

This comparison of the absurd and the serious helps to highlight these contrasts and encourage control in both situations. Their gross motor abilities will benefit greatly from playing this game.

Make the dancing a little harder to test control and emotional self-regulation even more. When dancing to rapid music, pick up the speed, and slow it down when dancing to slow songs. This brings in more stimuli, frequently a solution for emotional dysregulation.

Emotional dysregulation is a sophisticated way of describing a kids' emotional responses to circumstances outside the norm.

Additionally, it adds a new level of intricacy to the game, enhancing its enjoyment and interest. This game is particularly beneficial for controlling your emotions. To practice emotional self-regulation, children must respond to external stimuli and inputs.

Emotions and Situation Game Boards

With the help of this exercise, a referencing board with various emotions and feelings can be made. On the board, you will list several emotions and feelings, along with a tiny image or symbol representing each one.

This not only gives the activity a more game-like vibe, but it could also be more successful in helping your child visualize the feelings and emotions you want them to understand.

Ensure those emotions are represented on the board in various intensities if your child has trouble identifying a certain emotion.

For instance, if your child has trouble identifying and managing anger, you can write down multiple levels of anger on the board, such as unhappy, mad, furious, and passionate. This will make it easier for them to understand their emotions and emotional outbursts.

Chapter 5: Tolerate Stress and Deal with

Conflicts

Hey Kids!

Kids can endure a sudden emotional crisis by developing the ability to tolerate distress without getting it worse. When they feel powerless to alter the issue, they also assist them in accepting the reality of it. Distress tolerance abilities can aid kids in managing their emotions when they are unsure what they want or need. Dialectical Behavior Therapy (DBT) has a module called Distress Tolerance that teaches several skills.

Getting individuals to fulfill their obligations, carrying out your requests, and respecting your viewpoints are all objectives of interpersonal effectiveness. The goal is to improve existing relationships, create fulfilling new connections, and stop toxic or dysfunctional relationships. It's crucial to establish and sustain equilibrium in relationships and to strike a balance between change and acceptance.

Effective interpersonal skills must be learned; they do not come naturally. Building strong connections can frequently be hampered by emotions. Finding new relationships or ending unhealthy ones might occasionally be hampered by our automatic negative thinking about ourselves.

5.1 What are Distress Tolerance and interpersonal Effectiveness?

DBT strongly emphasizes developing coping mechanisms for pain because suffering is a natural part of life and cannot be completely avoided. Any time you change your behavior, you must be patient since impulsive behavior would get in the way. Distress tolerance is known as the capacity to accept one's surroundings without demanding that one change.

Distress tolerance techniques used in dialectical behavior therapy (DBT) address the propensity of some kids to find it difficult to cope with negative emotions. Low-tolerance individuals may become overwhelmed by even small amounts of stress and exhibit negative behaviors. The distress tolerance module of DBT teaches kids that there will be instances when pain cannot be avoided and that the most effective approach is to learn to accept and tolerate suffering. Many conventional treatment approaches place a strong emphasis on avoiding uncomfortable situations.

Radical acceptance is a crucial component of distress tolerance. When a kid cannot change the circumstance, this refers to accepting the circumstance and its truth. The kids will be less susceptible to strong and protracted unpleasant emotions if they practice radical acceptance without passing judgment or trying to reject reality.

Short-term coping mechanisms called "crisis survival skills" aid in controlling emotional suffering and preventing destructive actions. When experiencing intense emotional agony, they may take any action necessary to stop experiencing that suffering.

Examples of such behaviors are self-harming acts (cutting, burning, etc.), evading or fleeing the situation, abusing alcohol or drugs, or denying the existence of the stressor. Avoiding emotional discomfort might result in more dangerous or destructive actions, which could have detrimental long-term effects.

A kids' limbic system becomes activated and goes on high alert when they experience a real or perceived crisis. When a kid is upset, exercising adaptive coping skills is challenging.

A kid may be able to lessen the severity of their emotional suffering by using a distress tolerance skill. The individual can then apply additional DBT coping mechanisms, such as emotional control, mindfulness, and interpersonal abilities.

5.2 Distress Tolerance Skills

It's critical to be clear about your objectives and to respect yourself. DBT includes the following skill-building exercises to teach kids how to cope with stress and interact effectively with others:

Radical Acceptance

You may occasionally find yourself in a bad circumstance that won't improve. Acceptance will allow you to feel at peace and have the freedom to move on, even if you don't agree with it or enjoy it.

Radical acceptance recognizes that every one of us has a choice and that sometimes that decision is whether or not to recognize the reality of our circumstances. You have two options: either accept the circumstance and move on or continue to be miserable about it.

Imagine you have a fear of going to the dentist. You make an effort to disregard it. You attempt to refute it. But you are aware of your tooth decay. You and your previous dentist got along well, but he recently resigned. Your new dentist doesn't appear to have a good rapport with his patients and seems eager to use that pointy, whirling drill.

You'll probably start avoiding some of your favorite items that aggravate the cavities, such as sweets and frozen food, to avoid the dentist and manage the pain. However, that's okay, right? You've been considering increasing your intake of vegetables and seafood. That works out okay, save for when you eat an unidentified cavity irritant or when the discomfort in your cavities suddenly worsens.

By engaging in radical acceptance, you accept your fear of the dentist, the fact that seeing the dentist will be unpleasant, and the fact that the cavity must be filled. You cannot ignore it because if you do, a root canal will eventually be required, and nobody has time for that.

As a result, you arrive at the appointment prepared for the worst, but 45 minutes later, you leave with a full set of teeth and a renewed commitment to flossing. Let's not forget that you may utilize the skill set mentioned below to effectively navigate the dental chair with a suction tube hanging from your lip and the hygienist sprinkling water over your face.

Although practicing distress tolerance skills with DBT can appear intimidating, emotion regulation provides you more control over inclinations to act impulsively. You can enhance your mental well-being and capacity to endure upsetting circumstances regardless of whether you have a mental disease or personality disorder. You can hone these skills even more with the assistance of a DBT program or therapist.

Self Soothe

Utilizing your body's sensations in a critical situation is another easy technique to raise distress tolerance. The strength of negative feelings can be quickly diminished through sensory self-soothing.

Sight

Change your point of concentration by using your vision. Consider how many instances of a specific hue there are in the space, or concentrate on the texture of an object. You may also take out your phone and look through your preferred pictures.

Hearing

Observe sounds of any kind. Can you hear any chirping birds or nearby traffic? Listen to your favorite music with the volume turned up. You may install several apps on your cellphone to play relaxing music if that's what you want.

Taste

A modest pleasure can give you something enjoyable to think about as you struggle through a difficult situation. A bit of gum or a handful of mints will do; you don't need to make a full meal.

Touch

You may appreciate your sense of touch by feeling a pen in your palm, running your hands through your hair, or utilizing a fidget toy. You can cover yourself with a blanket or take a warm bath.

Smell

Concentrate on the aroma in the air, whether it's pleasant or unpleasant. Can you describe the smell or dissect it into its constituent parts? Put a few drops of your favorite lavender oil onto a cotton swab and carry it in a plastic bag for quick access to a scent you find comforting.

Movement

Although you only have five senses, in reality, DBT adds the sixth sensation of movement. Walk the block or dance to your favorite song since your body's actions can change your feelings.

Weighing The Pros and The Cons

Although this seems straightforward, we frequently make emotional decisions in times of crisis instead of logical ones. We want to leave the stressful situation as soon as possible because our body and mind are in "fight or flight" mode.

When we don't pause and properly consider our options, we could make snap decisions that have negative repercussions. A person should pause and take a minute to reason through their circumstances and the following steps before weighing the benefits and drawbacks.

When feeling very upset, making a list of the advantages and disadvantages of your goals may help you understand the reasoning. It is a technique for getting someone back to the DBT condition of a "wise mind" (middle path).

TIPP

TIPP is called temperature, Intensive Activity, Paced Inhaling, and Paired Relaxation Techniques.

TIPP techniques quickly relax the limbic system and reduce emotional excitation, usually between a few seconds to a few minutes. They have no negative side effects and can be done anywhere, including in public, unlike psychiatric medications. TIPP abilities can develop into a universal adaptive coping mechanism with practice.

TIPP abilities comprise:

- *The temperature*

The jolt of cold water shocks the body. If kids have trouble controlling their emotions, advise them to take a cold shower, spray cold water on their faces, or hold ice cubes in their hands.

Although these tasks won't harm the individuals, the cold weather will make it impossible for them to stay in a high emotional condition.

Intensive Exercise

Intense exercise adaptably alters the body's biochemistry, similar

to cold temperatures. The heart rate increases and the adrenaline is pumped during vigorous activity. A euphoric feeling is produced when the body is overloaded with adrenaline.

Paced Breathing

With timed breathing, tell the kids to take a slow, two-count inhalation via their nose, hold it for three counts, and then take a slow, five-count out halation through their mouth.

Paced breathing, which counts and regulates breathing, aids kids in regaining control by regulating their most fundamental biological function: breathing.

The kids will experience lower blood pressure, greater relaxation, and reduced tension when they learn to breathe softly and slowly. This can help with a variety of issues, including the impacts of anxiety, sleeplessness, and exhaustion.

Paired Muscle Relaxation

A pair of muscles, such as the feet on both legs, are tightened during inhalation and relaxed during exhalation in paired muscular relaxation (PMR). Work on the muscles from the top of the skull to the feet or the other way around.

THINK

A more recent DBT interpersonal effectiveness skill is THINK. It was created to lessen hostile feelings toward other kids. Although you won't always need to use this skill, it will come in handy when you're agitated and face interpersonal issues.

Consider the matter from the viewpoint of the opposing party. Is she also incensed? Does she think you're unreasonable in the same way you think she is?

Empathize with the other kids — How does it feel to be them? Allow yourself to experience her feelings briefly.

Interpretations of the actions of the other kids. Consider potential explanations for her behavior that may have angered you. Start with improbable justifications to get your mind thinking, then go on to more plausible justifications.

She wasn't born in a laboratory, but she works for one and does an experiment. Her dog passed away this morning, and she's trying to hide her grief by being unpleasant. She has issues with depression, and she recently had a meltdown that led to her being rude. She's also only human; she got upset and didn't handle it properly. Everybody makes errors.

Hopefully, these first three acts will help you control your anger to the point where you can think and behave more logically. The next two stages will be easier for you if you do that.

Take note of the other party. Take note of her attempts to be considerate and enhance the relationship. Even if you assume she has been crazy, notice that she appears scared. Even if you might not be on good terms yet, you should note that she has grinned at you. You only need to take note for the time being; there is no need to act.

Consideration in your reply. This does not obligate you to forget and forgive right away. This merely indicates that you used polite words. "What you said to me hurt, and I hope we can fix this in the future," you might respond. I require some space right now. Long-term relationships benefit more from a considerate answer than name-calling and ranting.

DEAR MAN

Whether or not you receive what you are requesting; using the DEAR MAN technique while requesting anything from another kid helps create and sustain a relationship.

Give a brief description of the circumstances. You may briefly summarize the circumstance by saying, "My buddies are going to see the latest superhero film this week," if you wish to go to the cinema with your friends.

Clearly state what you want. "I want to go to the movie with them," you say.

In a respectful and non-aggressive manner, make your point about why this is significant to you." Since track season has begun, I haven't been capable of spending much time with them, so I think it would be extremely significant if I could."

When you do receive what you have requested, reinforce it. "I swear before I go to the movie, I'll have my room tidy and my homework finished."

To be mindful is to remain present. Do not be concerned about the past or the future, such as what your friends may think if you cannot attend. Simply stay present.

Make a Good First Impression – Are you too nervous to ask your teacher for a question? "She must scold me if I asked help".

Approach the teacher no matter what, with assurance by thinking positively.

When it appears that you won't achieve your desired outcome during negotiations, be adaptable. Find a mutually beneficial middle ground through negotiation.

Kids frequently don't ask for things but instead make demands, ask indecisively, or don't ask at all and do as they please.

Anyone who wishes to improve their connections with those around them will benefit from learning interpersonal efficacy skills, not just those who struggle with borderline personality disorders.

5.3 Distress Tolerance Fun Activities

Dos and Don'ts

What to do OR not to do

What I need to do

What I Can't Control

What Is not my responsibility

Mantras

Stay in the moment

Don't think of the past

Don't think of the future

It is not my responsibility

I am not perfect

Everyone makes mistakes

I can't please everyone

Things I Don't Need to Do

Stress Triggers

My Stress Triggers

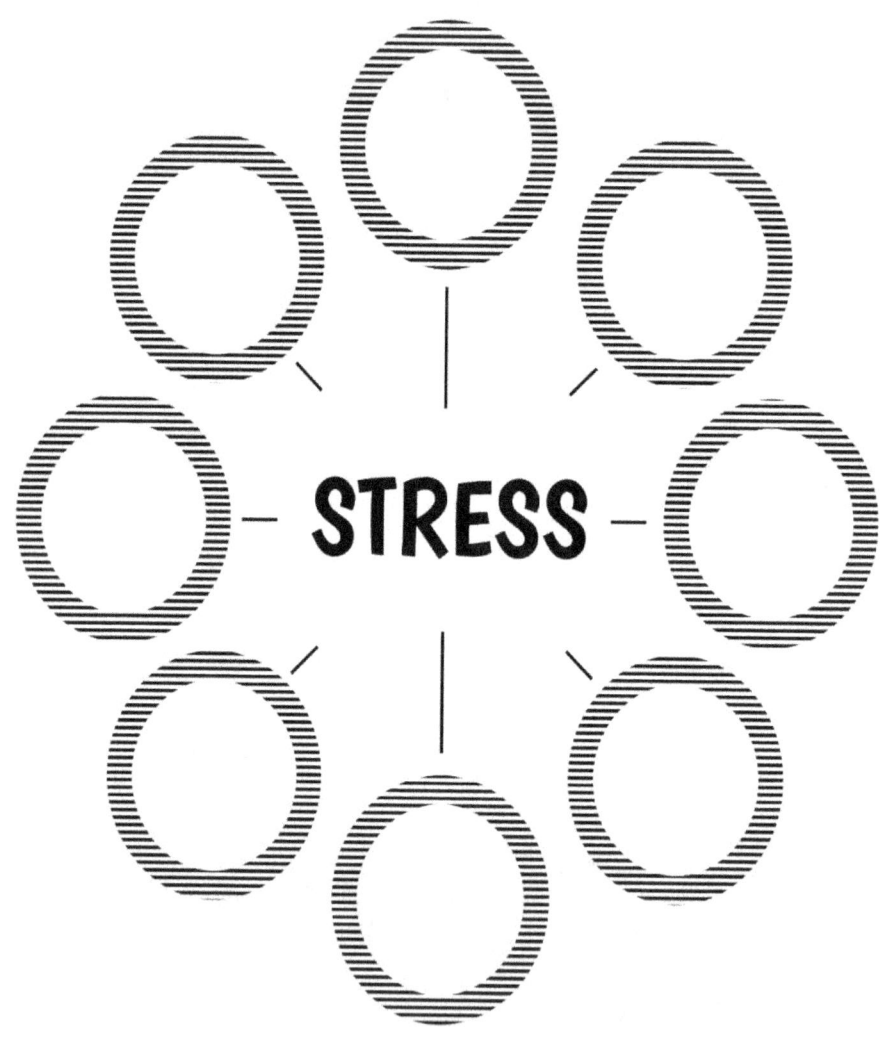

STRESS

Stress in My Day

Stress In My Day

When	What is stressing me	How it makes me feel	What I can Do
Before School			
In School			
After School			
In the Evening			
On the Weekend			

When I am Feeling Stressed

When I'm Feeling Stressed

I Can.......      I Should Not.......

BE ACTIVE KIDS
Don't Stress Out

```
R D K F P N U L H D E I P V V
M T W G W Z A E P Y L Q C R I
V R F W T P W T P Z I U L U T
H T A E R B D P U A M I F E D
Q V F K O B A T M R S T P S M
D V J O W H U C Z D E E V Y X
J M L A C E V R S K A N R B S
H U G S D M R W U C H A E Z V
V I S U A L I Z E L L C S E L
S L C N V S B W E L J T S R F
W T B A M X M Q K M E I Y T B
R P I E G P A B I P U V A W S
J E L L O A L H E R E E N Z
N L S Z L G Y R E H L U K F J
S E D T H I U Y F R M U S I C
```

ACTIVE	MUSIC	REST
BREATH	NATURE	SMELLS
CALM	PEACE	SMILE
HAPPY	PETS	STILL
HIKE	QUITE	VISUALIZE
HUGS	RELAX	YOGA

Chapter 6: Mindfulness: Learn to

Observe Thoughts

The advantages of mindfulness meditation have been extensively studied. Mindfulness techniques are considered essential for better emotion regulation in Dialectical Behavior Therapy (DBT). DBT mindfulness is introduced and reviewed throughout therapy, and mindfulness starts each skills training session. This is because mastering DBT mindfulness is a prerequisite for all other emotion regulation techniques in therapy. Although DBT mindfulness occupies a prominent position among DBT abilities, its ability to lessen emotional sensitivity and regulate emotions is sometimes misunderstood.

How do DBT and CBT incorporate mindfulness?

Emotional dysregulation is a condition that is treated using dialectical behavior therapy. Frequently, kids' perceptions of seemingly unimportant or trivial events trigger emotional dysregulation rather than the events themselves. You might, for instance, have a career in which you are reassuringly content. Say a clothing retailer employs it. It seems a wonderful fit because you enjoy dressing up and connecting with others. However, you don't enjoy folding laundry. You think it's dull. Now, a six-hour shift might only require you to fold clothes for around 30 minutes, which is only a minor percentage of the task. As you fold clothes, you could notice that your mind starts to think negatively about the act of folding garments. "This is awful." How time-consuming. This is foolish. This job is terrible.

Your mind is occupied with unsettling stories about this work, diverting your attention from folding the clothing. These stories will likely cause you to feel angry, resentful, or even depressed. What's worse, the remainder of your day tends to take on the color of these emotions. Now, instead of putting up with a tedious task for 30 minutes, you spend the entire day being negative about your job and feeling worse every minute. You start making judgments about your mood because, more often than not, being in a terrible mood for most of the day is quite uncomfortable, and you feel like you can't take it any longer. So much sorrow has resulted from something that was first rather minor.

To solve this problem mindfully, one could approach the unpleasant activity with an attitude of acceptance, willing to do it without passing too many judgments. As soon as you become aware of a judgment, you focus on folding the garments while being conscious of the feel of the fabric against your fingertips. Describe the new fabric's wavering scent as it comes to your nose. There is minimal room for unfavorable attributions when one fully commits to the topic and continually focuses their attention on it. Even now, you can discover it to be a relaxing hobby.

Making the best decisions is another area where mindfulness may be quite helpful. Many times in the past, kids who have persistent emotion dysregulation have invalidated their needs, wants, thoughts, and feelings. After some time, many who struggle with emotion dysregulation believe that their experience was false, harmful, or dangerous for some other reason.

Kids who become adept at disproving themselves frequently become disconnected from their own experiences. They no longer take their ideas into account. They are unable to locate their intuition any longer. Self-invalidators consequently lead lifestyles at odds with their ideals and aspirations. They don't think it matters when their needs are neglected in favor of someone else's. This leads to individuals who do not act in their best interests, which is a difficult way to live. They are consequently less content and more likely to experience emotional dysregulation.

Finally, mindfulness can assist in letting go of the struggle with unpleasant feelings, aiding emotional dysregulation. Kids trying to suppress or control their emotional reactions to things are one of the reasons they acquire emotion dysregulation. It's similar to attempting to hold on firmly to jelly when trying to manage your emotions. The more attempts you make, the messier it gets. When it comes to emotions, the more we attempt to control them, the stronger and more persistent they become. Unfortunately, there is pressure from the outside to control the feelings, which leads to more powerful emotions, more invalidation, etc., because of the atmosphere rife with invalidation from others. This frequently turns into a positive feedback loop.

6.1 What is Mindfulness in DBT?

Many of us have been considering resolutions for the Coming Year as the Christmas season ends. Do you want to take on a more active role in your life? Keep in touch with the friends you care about more. A better comprehension of oneself? There's a reason why you can't visit any health or lifestyle website without reading an article touting the advantages of mindfulness; doing so can help you make progress toward these overarching objectives.

What, then, is mindfulness? Being present in the now, without passing judgment, and not clinging to any particular moment can be described as a mindfulness. In dialectical behavior therapy

(DBT), we also define it as doing things non-judgmentally, doing one at a time, and doing what works for you (also known as "being efficient"). Being mindful is paying attention to the present moment, which encompasses all of your distractions, thoughts, and emotions, both good and bad. Narrowing your focus or focusing on one thing only are examples of this. Other times, mindfulness involves broadening your focus or paying attention to everything around you.

In DBT, it's necessary to learn and put skills, like mindfulness, into practice because it's believed that doing so will help kids get well and create lives worth living. There are numerous ways to cultivate mindfulness.

When someone consciously focuses their attention—and their awareness—those practices are known as formal mindfulness practices. For instance, paying attention to your breath might help you be mindful. You would do this by taking deep breaths in and out while focusing on how your body felt. What body parts sway while you breathe? How does the air feel in your mouth or nose? What is the rate of breath? Or, you may stroll sensibly down a trail through the woods. The noises of the environment around you, such as birds chirping in the trees above and leaves crunching beneath your feet, the fragrances of the vegetation and the outdoors, and perhaps even the sensation of some leaves or branches, can all be noticed.

While casual mindfulness exercises can be done anytime during the day, many kids use them to prepare themselves for informal mindfulness exercises. Being mindful is the process of recognizing these distractions and directing attention back to the meeting or the activity you're trying to engage in and focus on if you're having trouble focusing in a session and notice you're wondering about your to-do list for the day. Mindfulness does not (and should not!) "banish bad thoughts or emotions." As a result, DBT also teaches kids how to recognize their distress and unpleasant thoughts and sensations so they can deal with them more effectively or take action to assist them in passing through.

The following advice can help you incorporate mindfulness into your life this year:

Begin modestly. Select a habit that you already have. Try to keep it in mind. Start by doing it for a short time — even just a minute — at the start.

Exercise aloud. Pick up anything and speak aloud about it. What colors and textures do you see? What sensation do you have? What does it taste and smell like? Does it emit noises?

Being mindful means, by definition, being aware of your distractions. Our thoughts stray. It's not necessary to be thought-free or to have a clear mind to practice mindfulness. Being conscious of something happening is recognizing when our attention veers away from what we were being mindful of.

Don't evaluate your evaluation! You understand what I mean if you carry out this. Don't criticize yourself for distractions or judgments after noticing them. However, be aware, keep an eye out for it, and factually express how you judge yourself.

Don't be too hard on yourself, and *let go of the result*. Let it be what it is if you find this difficult or establish a goal but fail to achieve it. Sit with your current result and, once again, examine and describe it to yourself if the result of your new or growing mindfulness practice is not what you intended. Take note of your feelings about failing to achieve your goal. After that, make a new objective while you practice not hanging on to the present. Being mindful is another example of doing something repeatedly!

Daily Reflection Worksheet

About My Day

Today's Date:_____

My Mood	Today's Weather

Something I learned today:

_____

_____

_____

_____

3 things that made me happy today	3 things that I am grateful for today
1. _____	1. _____
2. _____	2. _____
3. _____	3. _____

Forgiveness Fingers

LOVE   ACCEPT   BREATHE

APOLOGIZE   LISTEN

Mindfulness
Scavenger Hunt
Relax and Focus on The Moment

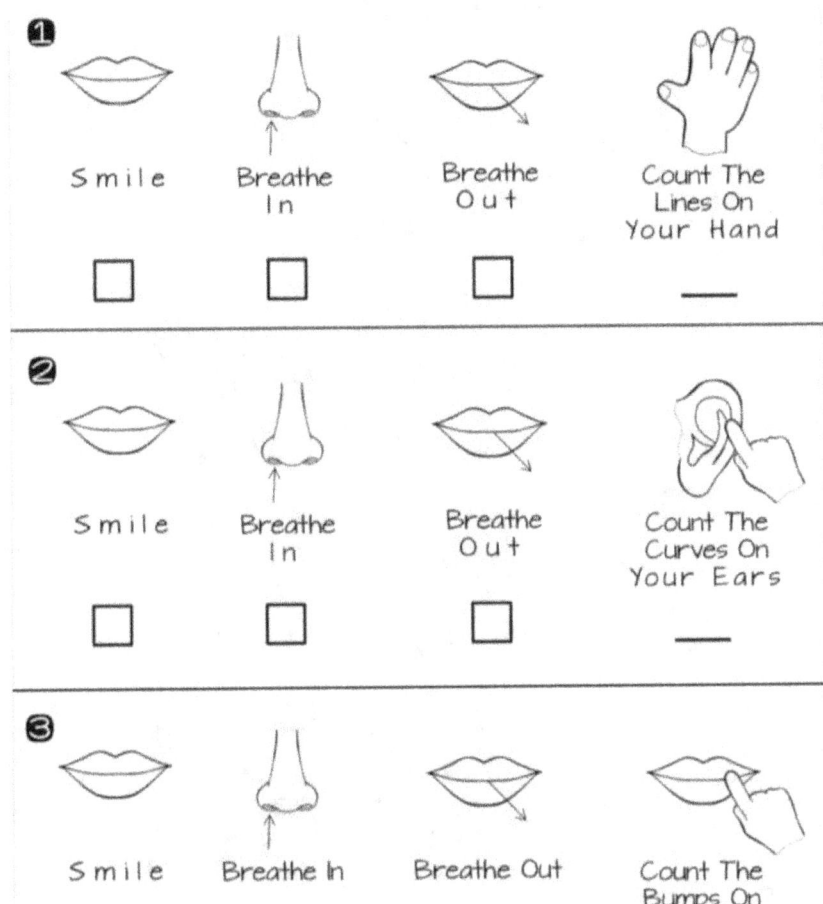

①

Smile ☐ Breathe In ☐ Breathe Out ☐ Count The Lines On Your Hand ___

②

Smile ☐ Breathe In ☐ Breathe Out ☐ Count The Curves On Your Ears ___

③

Smile Breathe In Breathe Out Count The Bumps On Your Lips

Mindfulness Bingo

find something smooth	find a flower that smells good	find something hard
notice the color of the sky	find something that is your favorite color	make someone laugh
listen to a song you love	help a family member	give someone a compliment
find something soft	feel the grass under your feet	find something bumpy

Trace and Breathe

Trace along the rainbow with your finger as you breathe in and out

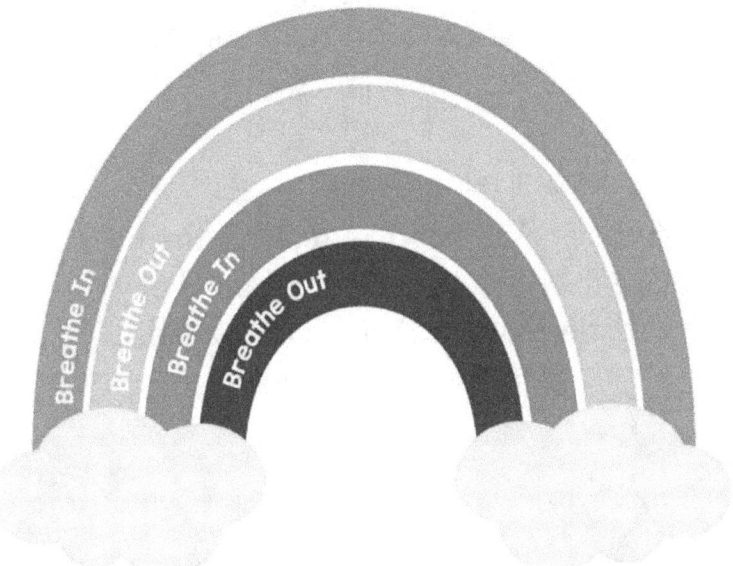

5-4-3-2-1 Mindfulness
List...

5 things you can see
4 things you can touch
3 things you can hear
2 things you can smell
I thing you can taste

HEART BEAT EXERCISE

Ask your child to stand up and either
jump up and down or do jumping jacks
for one minute.

At the end of that minute, have them
place their hand on their heart and pay
attention to how their **heartbeat** and
their **breathing** feel.

KIDS YOGA EXERCISE POSTER

SEATED POSES

SALUTATION SEAL 2

COW FACE POSE

SEATED FORWARD BEND

SALUTATION SEAL

COW FACE WITH EAGLE ARMS

SEATED TWIST POSE

EASY POSE

SEATED FORWARD BEND

REVERSE PRAYER

6.4 Promote Self-Regulation in Child Development

Let's look more closely at how parents and daycare providers may encourage self-regulation in environments where children are developing now that we've discussed the significance of self-regulation in child growth and the role that caretakers can play.

Create Wholesome Connections

Creating a good rapport with kids paves the way for developing self-control abilities. This starts with the caregiver realizing that children who struggle to focus or regulate their emotions are not "bad kids" or "out of control" rather they are the children who require extra help and attention to learn self-regulation.

A trusting and caring relationship can be established, which serves as a foundation for the growth of self-regulation abilities when caregivers provide support through warm and receptive interactions, constructively addressing problem behaviors, and offering physical and emotional solace when a child is upset.

Organize Your Environment

The growth of self-regulation in children requires a gradual succession of demanding conditions, just like other skill development. By providing a structured setting intended to encourage the development of self-regulation skills, caregivers can help this progression in the context of child development.

Caretakers should create a pleasant atmosphere without supporting off-task behaviors to create a well-organized learning environment that effectively promotes self-regulation.

- Ensure ideal air and lighting, and noise levels.
- Reduce distractions and encourage children to concentrate on their work using walls and separators.

- Control the environment's traffic flow to reduce unnecessary distractions.
- Desks and tables should be arranged in task-appropriate arrangements.
- Educate Children on the Big Picture of Goal-Achieving

Self-regulation is the capacity to regulate emotions and behaviors to enable goal-directed actions, as described above. By assisting children in identifying goals, establishing their own goals, and understanding how self-controlling their impulses and emotions will help them reach those goals, caregivers can enhance children's development of self-regulation. This is particularly true for children who are having trouble developing impulse control.

Practice Optimal Discipline

Children and adults with self-regulation abilities can accomplish their goals while simultaneously avoiding the negative effects of inappropriate behavior. Children need to understand the repercussions of their actions as their cognitive development progresses to make wise decisions.

Our caregivers are responsible for creating a controlled environment with predictable rules and penalties. Instead of using sanctions that breed resentment and have limited long-term effectiveness, positive discipline aims to solve behavioral difficulties via respect for one another, problem-solving, and personal responsibility.

Teach Self-Control Techniques

Kids who haven't mastered coping mechanisms for intense emotions may engage in "acting out" activities like yelling, disrupting others, or throwing tantrums. Positive self-regulation techniques and emotional coping mechanisms should be taught to children by parents and daycare providers to stop these behaviors.

Kids can learn to manage strong or uncomfortable emotions by using straightforward coping mechanisms like deep breathing, counting to 10, going for a walk, or journaling. Self-distraction, concentrating on something else, playing a game in your head, or getting more exercise during the day are all effective methods for behavioral self-regulation and impulsive behavior. Playing games and other activities that appropriately test a child's ability to pay attention, utilize creativity, follow directions, and manage urges helps kids develop executive function.

When caregivers can have a happy attitude and be patient while giving children the guidance, structure, and encouragement, they require to grow in their ability to self-regulate, they can truly make a difference.

THE BOTTOM LINE

It is tempting to characterize difficult behavior as rebellious, attention-seeking, manipulating, and aggressive. However, children's difficult behavior is frequently out of their control. Understanding this conduct as a sign that children cannot control their strong emotions is more accurate and useful. When someone is feeling overwhelmed, their emotions take control. They are, therefore, unable to self-regulate.

Children need to be encouraged to develop the skill of self-regulation since it is essential to their overall success and enjoyment. Children who can control their emotions—such as tension, rage, disappointment, and frustration—do better in class, with their friends, and at home. Keep in mind that kids will find it simpler to deal with and adjust to change the more they learn self-control. Children can benefit from removing unneeded demands and caring guidance and support.

Everyone manages emotions in their unique way. Some people acquire the ability to handle difficult situations as children, while others never do. Kids who need to enhance their crisis coping skills can be taught distress tolerance abilities as a module in dialectical behavior therapy. An expert can teach DBT skills using a variety of materials. Kids who experience extreme distress may behave impulsively, but when they practice emotion regulation techniques, they regain their "wise mind" and can make better choices. You shouldn't need to be DBT certified to help any patient with realistic coping skills if you use the tools and advice provided in this book. So try these strategies and worksheets and provide us with your valuable feedback.